DESIRES TO REMEMBER

DESIRES TO REMEMBER

A COLLECTION OF POETRY AND ART

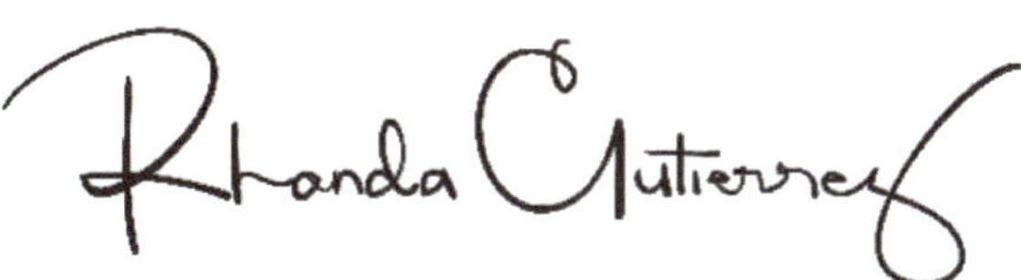

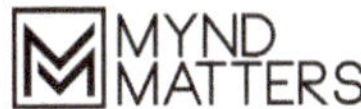

MYND MATTERS

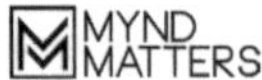

PUBLISHED BY MYND MATTERS®

For information about bulk orders or special sales, please contact the publisher at www.myndmatterspublishing.com or 888-833-2548.

ISBN: 978-1-963874-36-5 (pbk)
ISBN: 978-1-963874-37-2 (hdcv)

FIRST EDITION

Author Photo by Derek C. Kearney

Painting is silent poetry, and poetry is painting that speaks.

—Plutarch

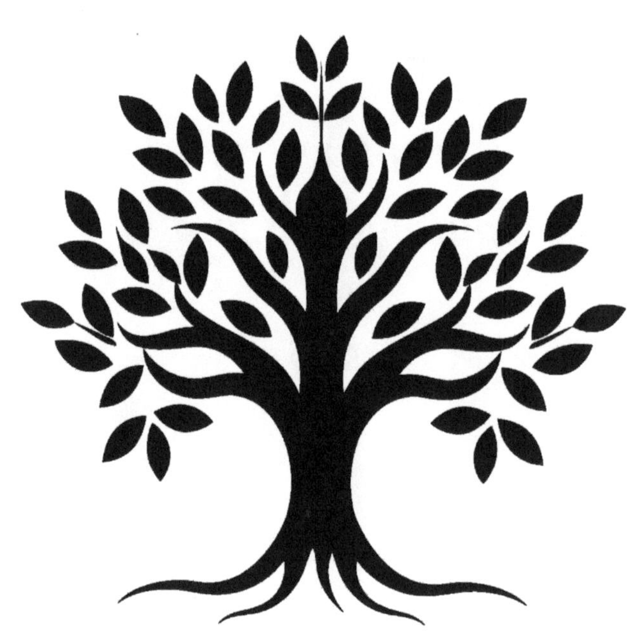

To My Family

To my biggest fan, my dad, Richard Gutierrez:
You have always inspired me to take risks, not be afraid of change, and value going after my dreams,
Thank you for your endless encouragement and love.

To my shero, my mom, Rosa Zayas:
You are the pillar of strength and possibility. Thank you for being our spiritual compass and teaching me that serving
others is the greatest way to connect and make a difference.

To my brother Rick: may we always stand shoulder to shoulder as we succeed in our dreams.
Your positive attitude in life is only a reflection of the great heart that you have,
Thank you for reminding me to always laugh with and at life.

To my bonus sister Rose: your love for the family is heartfelt.
Thank you for always saying yes with open arms and the greatest smile ever.

To my sister Raquel: you may never know the depths of the life lessons received
from the courage, love, and tenacity I have witnessed through your life's journey.
Thank you for showing me true grit.

To Winnieveruschka, Jennifer, Ricky Jr., Stephanie, Jonier, Amanda, Omar, Daniel,
Leslie, Junior, Syann, Ayana, Mayson, Mila, Liam, Rowan, River, Alexis, Lucas, Adrian, and Luna.
This book is especially for you: Go after every dream, every goal,
and every wish. Always remember that everything you want to Be, you already are.
I will always be here for you...whenever and for whatever.
Your Titi Rhonda.

To Maddie and Bella, whose warmth, companionship, and love I could never repay, even
with a lifetime of dog treats, but I will try.

I love you all immensely.

FOR THE ART OF HEALING

Music, dance, writing, storytelling, collage-making, photographing, and painting can be all employed as art therapy. The freedom of artistic expression is not measured by the quality of the art produced, but instead by the process of artistic creation.

Healing through the arts is used for mental, emotional, and physical conditions improving the way we feel. A liberating sense of inspiration frees us from the mundane when we express ourselves in any one of the countless art forms. When we sit still long enough to experience being present to feel who we truly are, allows for discovering our state of grace.

Healing through the arts opens an avenue through which we more clearly communicate our emotions. Our brains are loaded with serotonin during the creative process, we feel motivated and inspired to love and seek peace. I recall how each creative endeavor, whether it was painting, photography, or poetry, always filled my heart. I had found a form of wordless communication structured by my inner being.

Discovering, channeling, and owning my artistic muse has been a journey of self-discovery where surrendering to it frees me from any seeming dis-eases.

CONTENTS

CONTENTS

*Art washes away from the soul the dust
of everyday life.*

—Pablo Picasso

FOREWORD

What do we do with our pain? Do we conceal it? Do we suppress it? Do we weaponize it and use it as a battering ram? What do we do with our loss? Do we internalize it? Do we allow it to swallow us up whole? Do we ruminate on it, and let it lead us to places of self-pity?

What do we do with our memories, the good ones, the bad ones, and the in-between ones? Do they stale in a musty closet, decaying in files we are too afraid to revisit? Do we sit with them and let them sit with us but make no meaning of those moments passed?

How do we catalog the many visions and versions of ourselves? The good and the not-so-good versions of ourselves? And how do we reconstruct all of the ways that we've loved and been loved, betrayed and been betrayed, hurt and been hurt, healed and been healed, played and been played, forgive and been forgiven? And who would benefit from such a collection if we were to salt down the bitter, the salty, and the sweet lessons of a well-seasoned life?

Who better to answer these questions than the one who bravely paints with the colors of her soul transforming word imagery that is both abstract and concrete?

Who better than the woman who voluntarily drenches herself in life's crucible, so that we may all be shown how to gather the fractals of our storied lives and transmute them into art?

And this, dear gentle reader, is what you will encounter as you glimpse into a living mosaic of one woman's well-gathered life.

To get the full value of this collection, I urge you to find an in-distractible space where you can sit down with these words and let them search you, find you, forgive you, and free you. Savor these sacred writings by reading them deliberately and out loud. Lose yourself in the accompanying original images and see if you can't find a common thread of your own story.

It will be at that time that you will come to encounter and appreciate the ways your journey intersects with that of my 3 am friend, artist, photographer, and poetic priestess, Rhonda Gutierrez, and like her, you will find something holy in the colors of your soul.

— Kevin Kitrell Ross, BA, MRPL, DD

PREFACE

De / sires   / to /   Re / member
(from) (Lord)   (movement toward)   (Again) (be mindful of)

Desires to Remember is a constant longing to stay mindfully conscious of who I am amid life's experiences. Spiritual forgetfulness is common, a calling to remember from the voice within is my heart's true desire.

For every heart that gets to heal through the magical power of art, may you find the artist within to create the life you deserve.

INTRODUCTION

For as long as I can remember, I have been attracted to various artistic endeavors: arts and crafts, dance, poetry, photography, and painting. I vividly recall being inspired as a teenager to compose a poem and to my surprise, my submission won first prize in my high school talent contest. That was a moment of self-realization—my epiphany—that I was good at something. This revelation excited me, as I used words born of heartbreak and life challenges to express my deepest desires and greatest fears.

I have long been fascinated by the study of human behavior. This led to reading books that offer insights into why we behave as we do. This exploration of our psyche prompted me to embark on a spiritual journey that gave me a fresh perspective on my personal growth and development. Grappling with philosophical principles that delve into life's most profound questions opened my mind to a new realm of creative possibility. Of all my artistic endeavors I gravitate most toward abstraction. I feel that the most profound way to connect with others through an artistic medium is to allow them to interpret what they experience for themselves.

Poetry, in particular, holds a special place in my heart. I am enamored by its ability to breathe life into words, to convey the intensity of pain, love, and human experience. It was the works of Puerto Rican poet Julia De Burgos, specifically her poem "Rio Grande de Loiza," that initially sparked my love for poetry. I yearned to write with the same depth and power as she did, leading me to seek other poets who have inspired me over the years. One poet who resonates deeply with me is Emily Dickinson, She believed that poetry achieves relief, and personal identity, and helps communicate the urgency of doubts and the need to find faith.

Over time, I have also delved into the world of abstract art and photography, finding immense joy in them, yet poetry will always remain my first love. This book, which was conceived long ago, chronicles my experiences of loss, love, desire, ego, and life, but above all, it reflects my quest for self-mastery. Along the way, I discovered that self-mastery is an illusion, but awareness and consistent practice to stay present leads to detachment and joy. While much of my poetry may seem to be about specific individuals or situations, I am fully aware that each person and experience merely serves as a reflection of my current state of consciousness and understanding. I hope that you delight in the sharing of those moments.

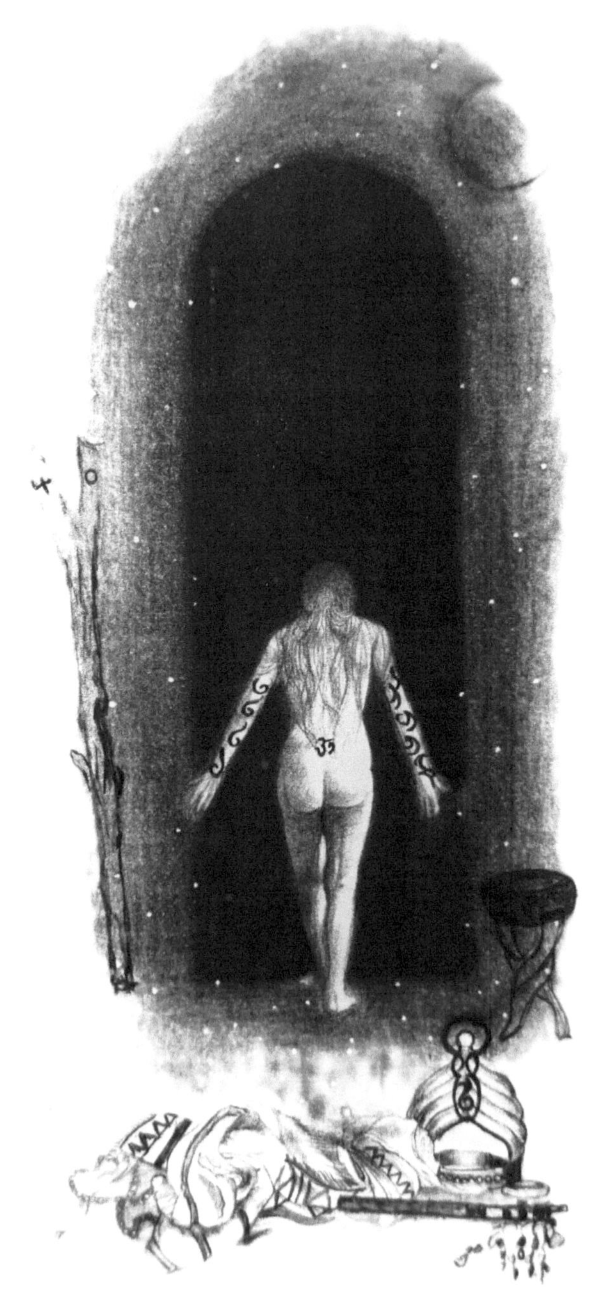

THE WILDERNESS

For every shared moment, every kept secret,
there is a vivid memory stored.
In my solemness, I have sighed at the birth of words
brought together in an expression of times before.

I will forever keep embedded in my heart, those who have shared themselves,
leaving behind new beginnings,
knowing traces of me live in their experience.

I smile briefly as images of lost love enter my pensive days.
and laugh softly at trails of tears that linger.

I write of the hours spent in gatherings, seeking
a place to rest the thoughts that challenged me and packed my bags
to see about a council of spirits
that shared time in precious recluse.

Walking into infinite possibilities, I stand before
these memories, the ages of experiences that have
connected me to something greater than myself.

The scarring of this soul's endless journeys,
marked with symbols from ancestral branches guided me
through this heart's tender course.
With open arms, I walk straight into the wilderness,
40 days carrying nothing but this naked instrument
pressing through mysteries of the unknown.

Guided and safe under a wing of remembrance,
the words I write and now surrender
have become my desire to remember.

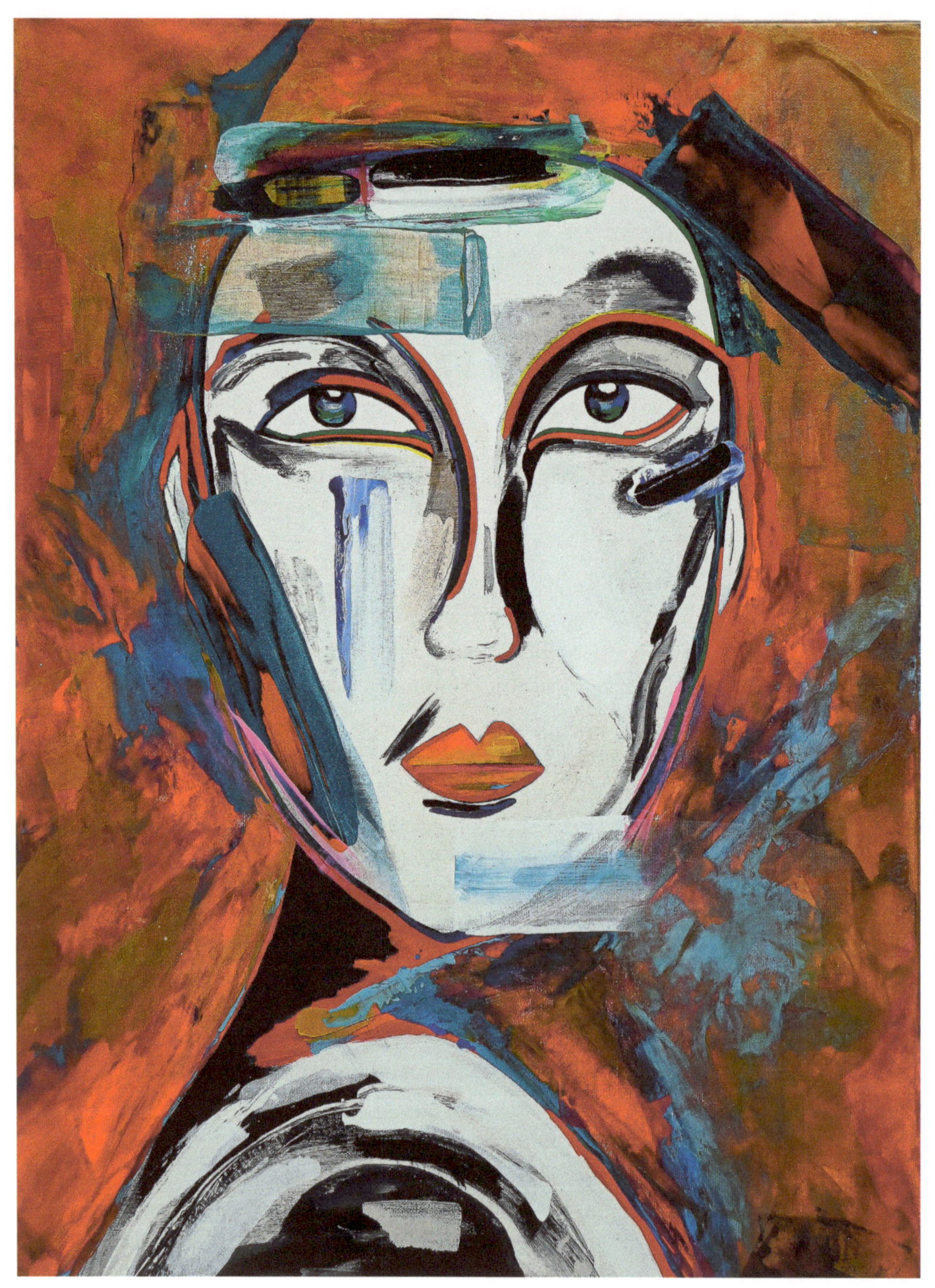

WHO WILL TAKE CARE OF ME

The days go by in a blink and my body feels weary from catching up to yesterday's dreams.
I feel like there is so much time being wasted on repeated lessons and cries out to be seen,
that peace and silence are my only waking constant desire.

Have I done enough, served enough, cared enough, rescued enough?!
Have I not transformed enough that my plea for understanding is my song of worth, and at times I
don't know the difference between feeling joy and being valued?

Stretching moments from comfort to experience the now is the light that is saving me, the grace
that keeps me awake and present. Yet it is at times a tug of war between solitude and connection,
between sanity and empathy for humanity. Knowing you are loved without feeling loved,
filling my cup, and craving they notice I need water.

Letting go of attachments while looking for resolve, seeking the joy of stillness and
witnessing my coming and going in circles.

I am strong yet preoccupied with exhaust and being incredibly blessed yet still torn.
Decay is real and each minute is unforgiving and jealous of the next, complacency can wrap its
warm throw around me, and I never feel its sneer.

Every year I hear the resounding "I should know better" whispers in my head
for each time I vote to drain my soul with fear dressed like rage,
and loneliness clothed with indignation.

It's easy to name this feeling of sadness and despair giving into the story of losing out on my
goals, my talents, and unconditionality for those who I would die for but judge so harshly.

Who will care for me, even as I wander off? Who will care for me when I don't care at all? And the days disappear
without warning and I am left standing and wondering. Did you ever see me, did I ever see me?
Have I lived enough, loved enough, cared enough?

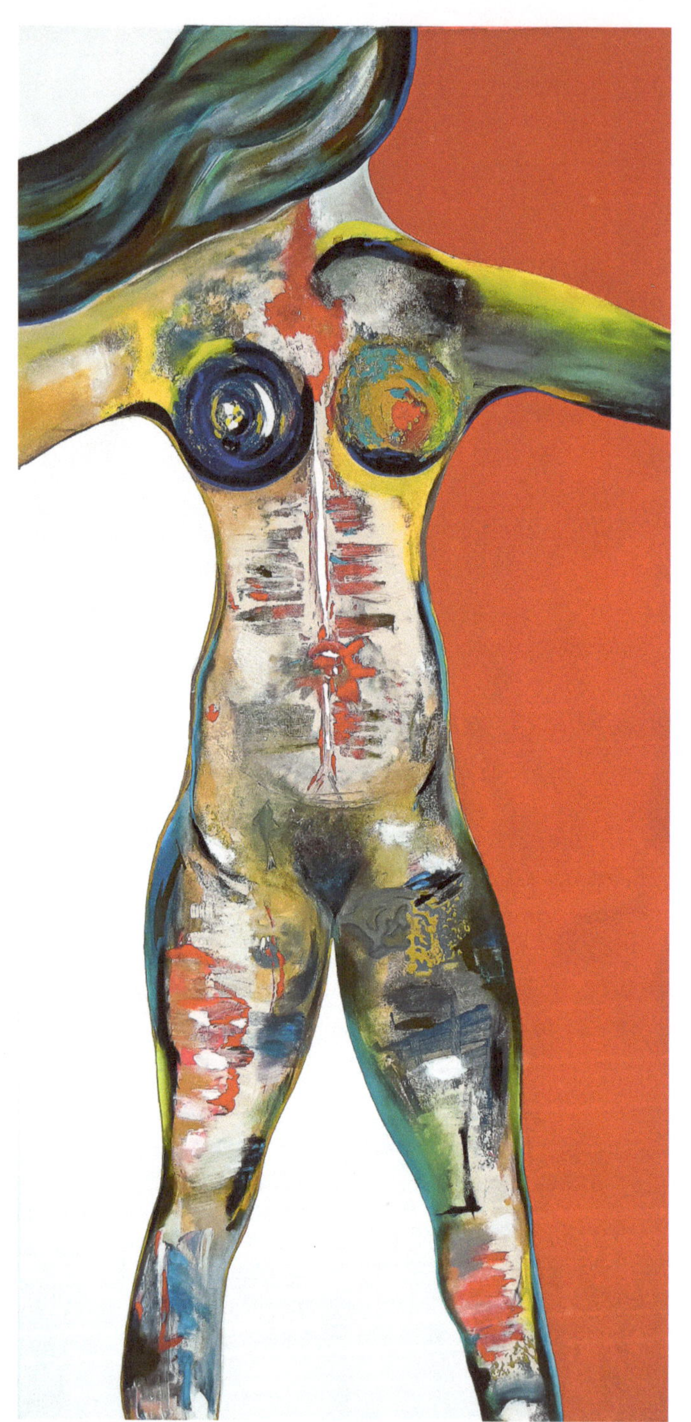

URGENCY

The hourglass sand is dropping,
Awakened to the air flowing through the day.
Make accounts for the minutes spent on purpose.
Blanket your soul with accomplishment.

Today is the day you seize that thought,
that life-transforming thought.
Today, recognize the nature of truth principles,
and practice a pledge that honors you.

Rise to your greatness and all the
deadening past is quicksand.
Rise to the talents bestowed
and call forth the spiritual beings.

Then Be Still and Know.

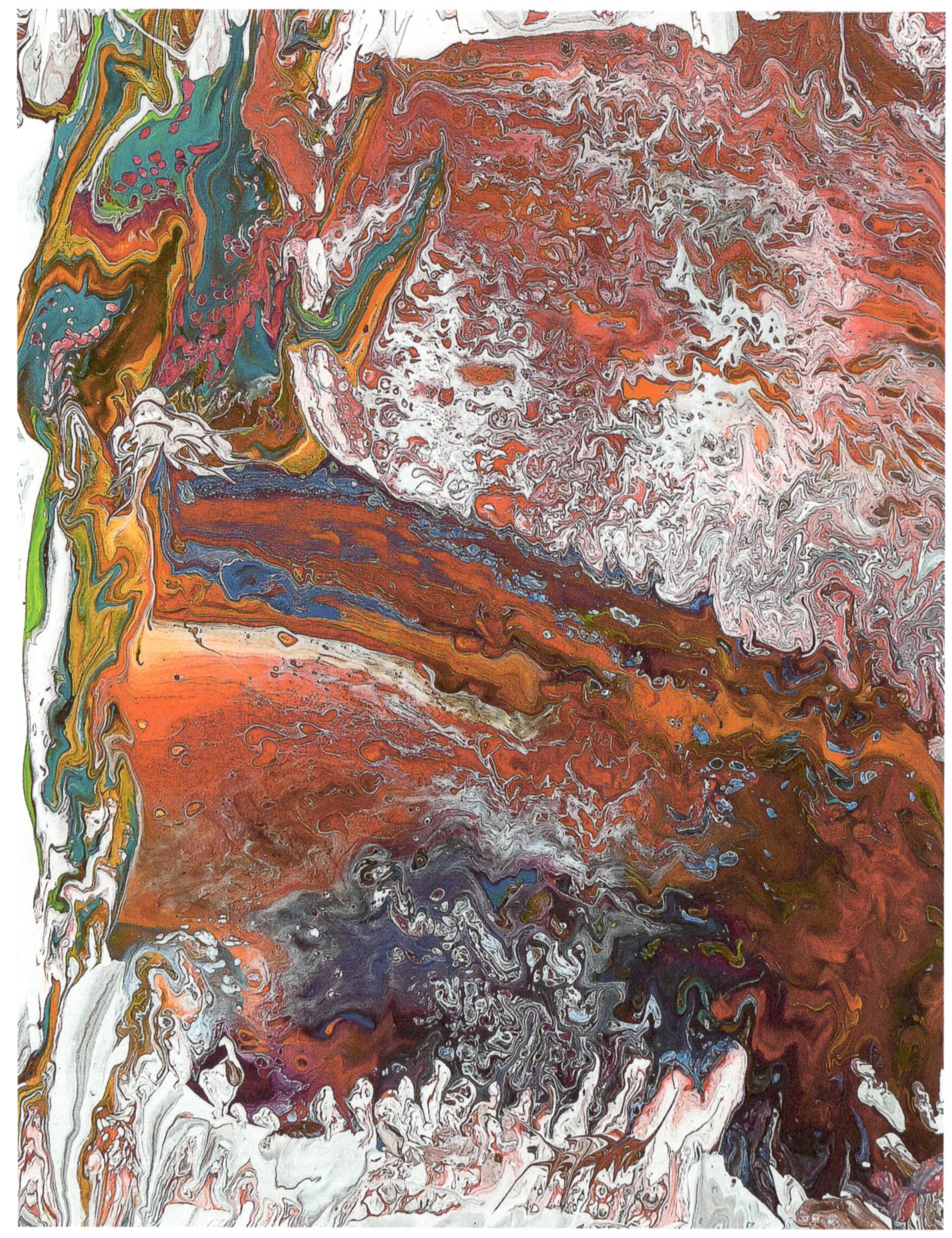

MYSTICAL ROARS

Feeling my floating body caress the aromatic winds
I learned to breathe new air that cleanses my soul.
My stained feet imprinted satin sands with traces
of jeweled treasures that grandfathers left behind.

Toasting to chanting melodies
shadows dancing along the moonlit waters.
I can still hear the vibrating
echo from the morning bell,
how perfect the sound of
mother nature's mystical roar.

Lifting spirits and healing possibilities,
I welcome the serenity my master's
home has brought me.

The tides wash away unwanted memories,
my skin painted with the ooze of an ancient bath
circling along the almighty sun aligning
with earth's vibrant energy
the desire to never go back enters my mind.

Inspired by an escape into the Costa Rica Forest at Nozara's retreat.

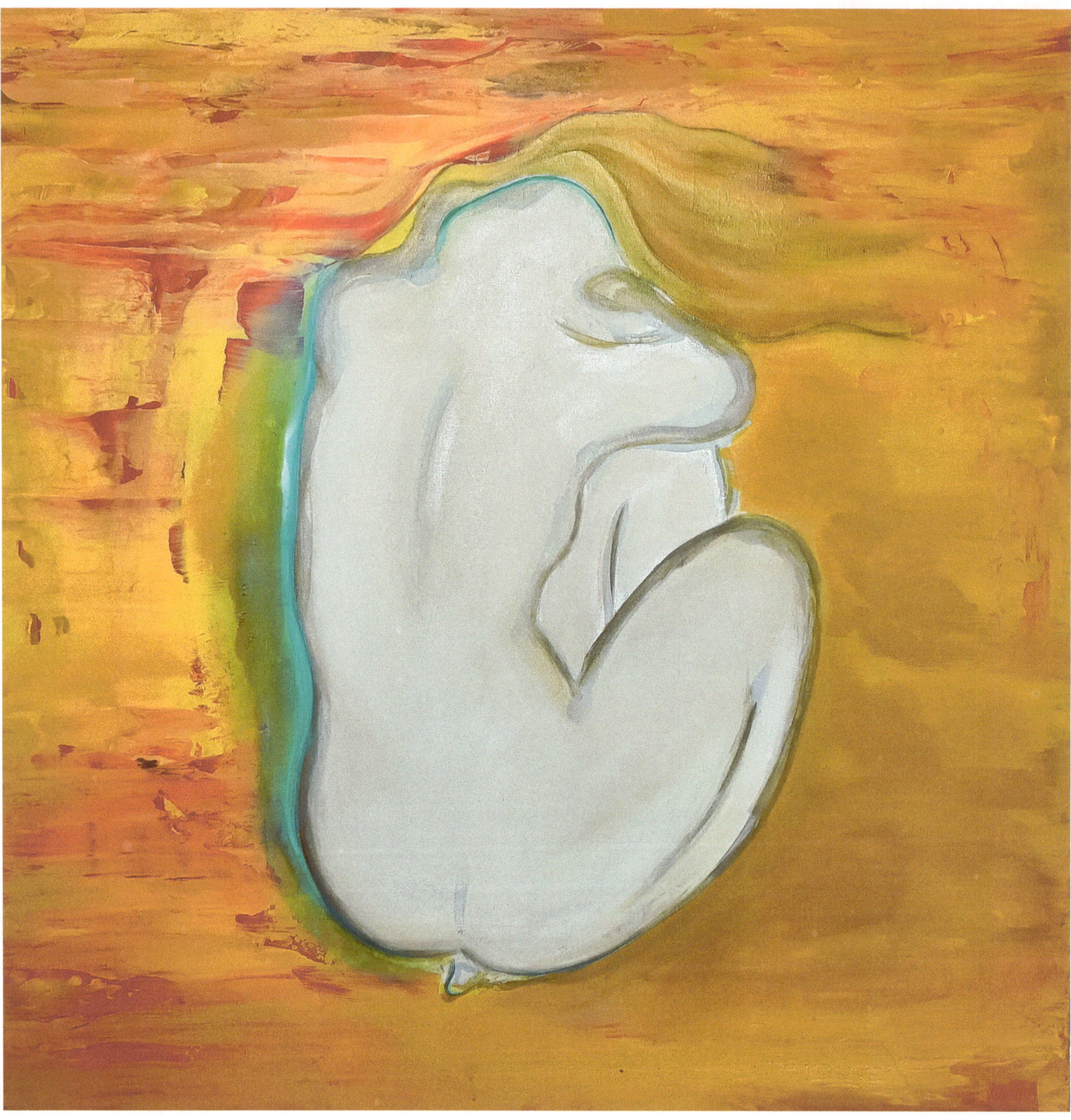

WITNESS

A flame of lavender aids the mind
the escape of suffocated judgments.

It's longing for resolve exhausted from
Endless thoughts of rambling.

It can see her Lotus frame
quivering as the mind taunts
a space where freedom seeks its dawn,

and the self dissolves
because it never stood a chance.

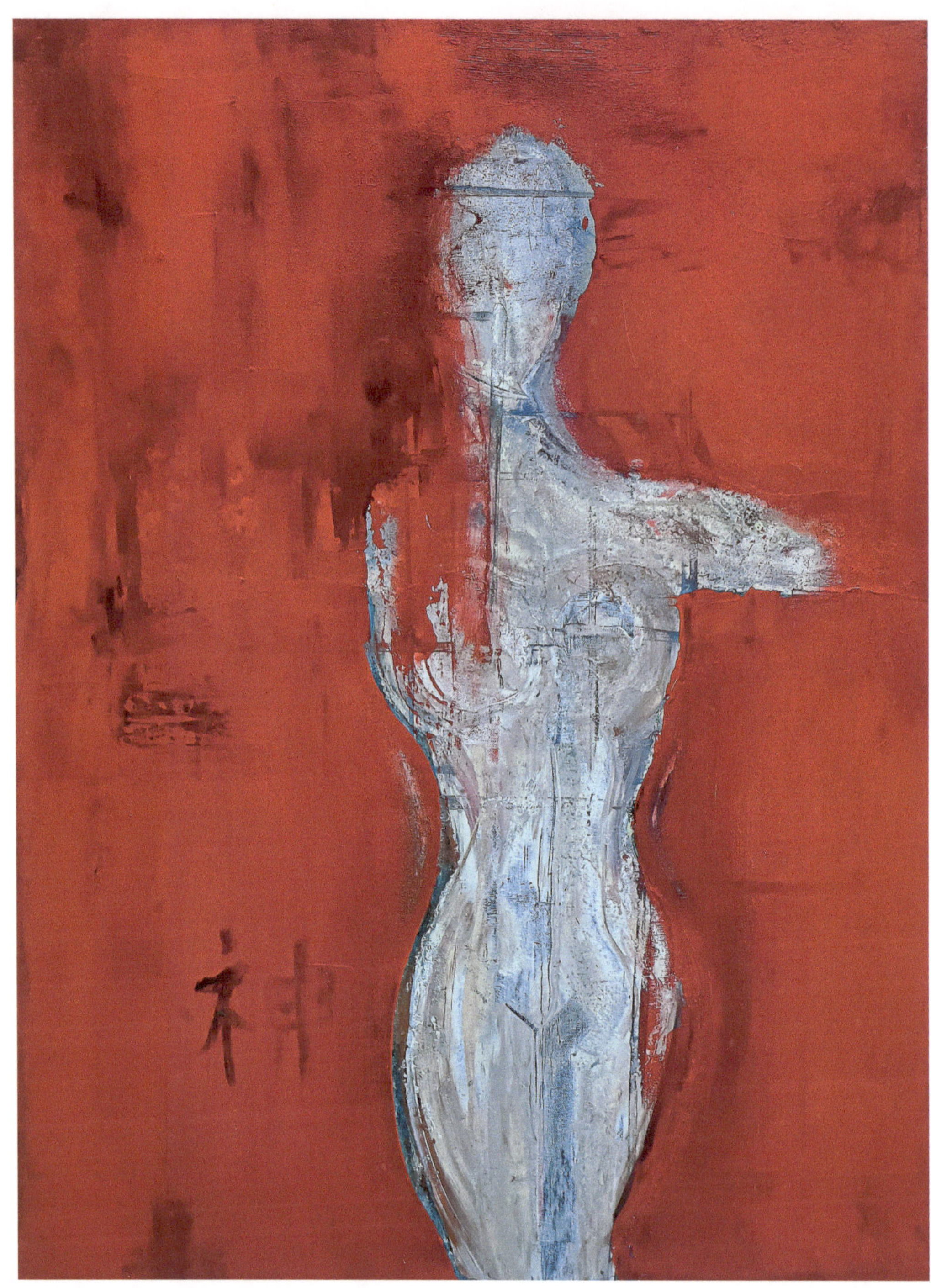

RAGE

Her laughter is heard echoing from
behind the two-way mirror.
Driven by currents of bad blood that thicken.
Crumbled by spirals of fire set in her eyes,
she is unreached,
drafted into the house of demons,
now no one is heard, only the rusted skeletons.
She walks right through the walls,
invisible to our pain and shadowed by her convictions.
She is dried out and exhausted, drained by righteousness,
unwilling and defenseless, we become.
Soon, we will be free of the
rage that governs us.

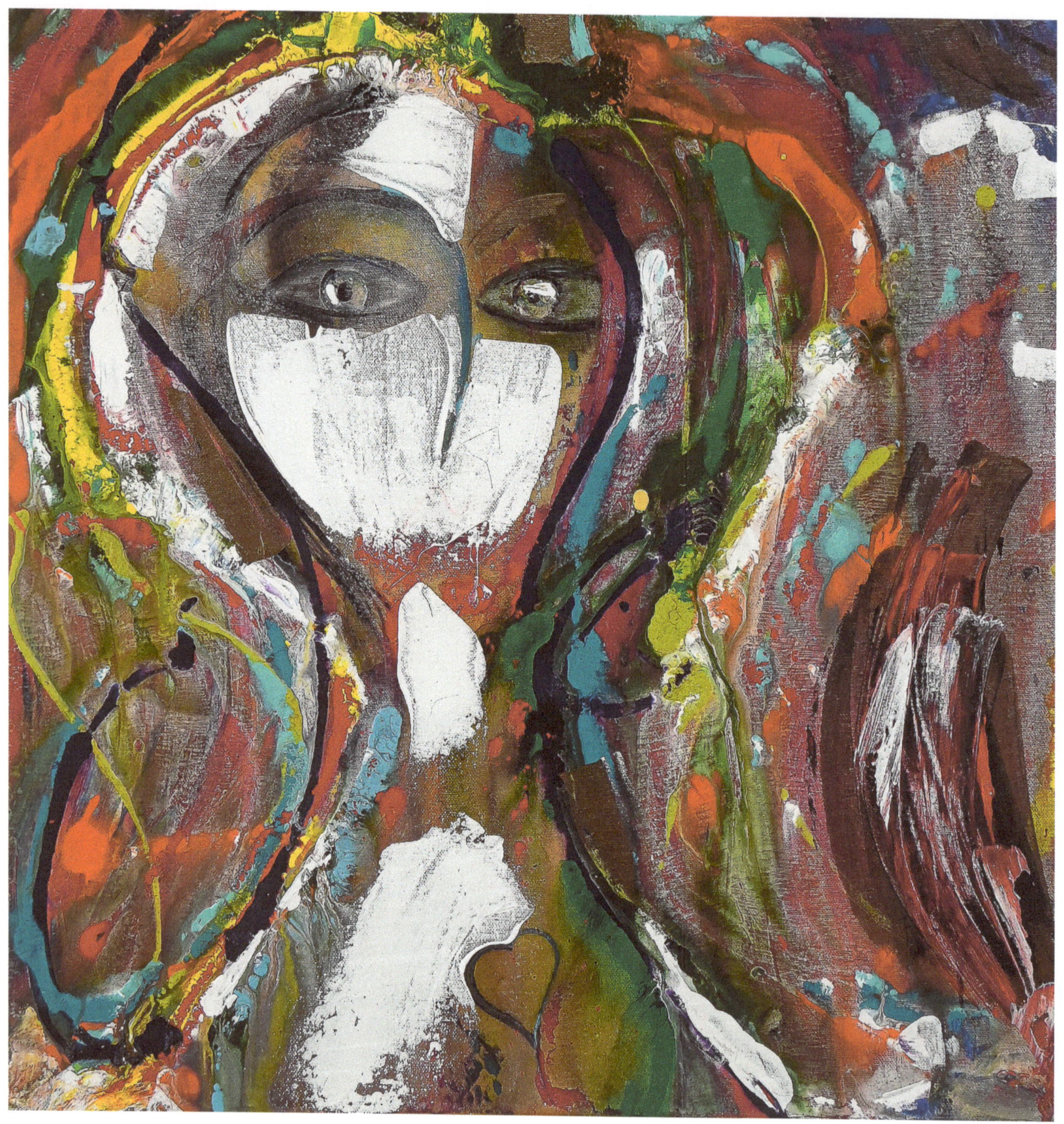

PRIDE

I am the reflection of my Ego's fears,
the one who sits content
in silence breathing polluted air
that floats calmly in the absence of words.

I am obedient to the thoughts that resound from the realm of a lower consciousness.

Paralyzed, I do not stretch my heart to reach yours, that would be to surrender
to let go.

Instead, I hold on to a familiar pain that
separates me from my good.

THE HEM

Do not miss me as you walk the hills of foreign lands.
Do not invite me into thoughts of solitude
nor during the waves of noises in your head.

Do not imagine our romance to drinks of
wine that you envision in my absence.

For I stood there blowing you blessings,
as you departed into yourself again and again.

Left behind to read a slurred heart from
cities, temples, circles, and paradise.

Be careful of the safety that lies with walking
to the pace of a sought-after man.
Distracting you from your true assignment.

The cup of cool water runs over you
in a journey that circles the marathon of voices,
at a finish line of applause that does not exist.

Your heart pulls from the earth, calling to
reign over the trouble.
Hear the choir of Seraphim
sing a beautiful hymn of the elevated
consciousness that humbles the already meek.

I am nothing in your path but a pool to reflect upon.
I am nothing in the lifetime
crowds of words that you will deliver.

I have nothing for you to think of or imagine.
I am your North and your South,
your smile, and your sadness.

I am where you carry me to and probe
in the deepest of your wells when invited.

To you, I exist in the perfection of someday.
Yet, I am here standing, undisturbed by
the familiar known which is safer to write about.

When you shed the secrets of sacredness,
feel the cradle of faithful, draw from the ages of
resounding hearts of your incarnations,
turn to the one that touched your robe,
there you will find healing.

Dedicated to Keboo

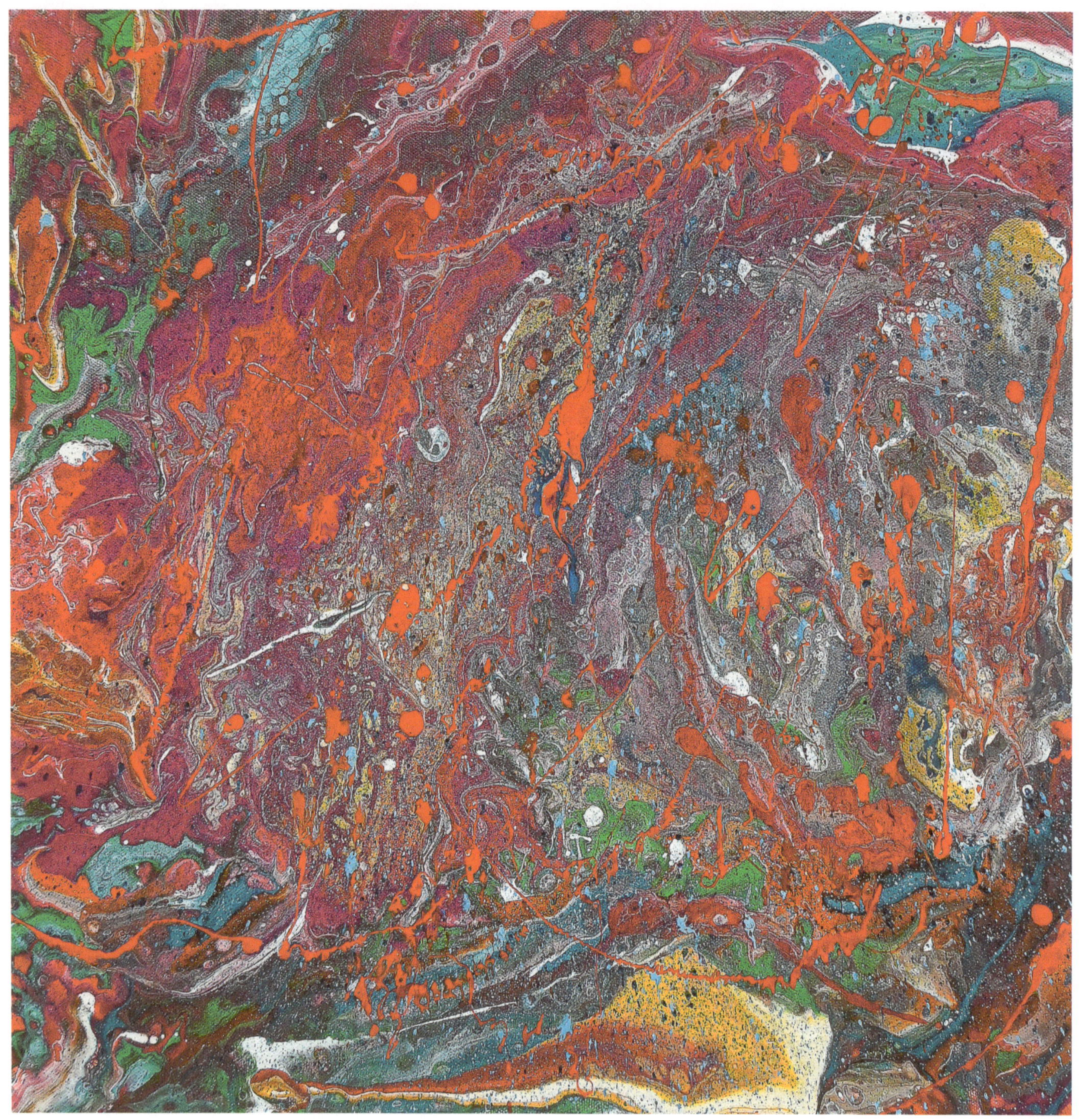

GODSENT

Pretty are the collected dried roses,
air-tight memories corked and safe
from the cheap cheated thrills, like streams of light,
dimmer than a flare gun.

Picking away the fallen chips of fire
that scabbed my skin and scarred me.

I promised myself no more driven luxuries
or half-ass gifts with green labeled bottles.

To the million men, who call themselves masters,
warriors who walk in wonder,
overheated by their demons:

Don't let the glass cut you deep
if you find your way, walk on water to the other side.
I will be watching you heal
your way through the crosswinds.

A BOY

A boy trotting his feet to a generational rhythm,
he sets the stake, a sacred grounding for his
brothers to come.

The heart of a great man settles inside this small-frame child.
A child of new thoughts dancing with his soul honoring
the mothers through a sweet vibrational harmony.

The boats sailing on winds ignited, fires burning
for the healing of men before him.

I know that this is how the earth is nourished by
the little ones that are born into the mansion of
an almighty existence.

I was there to witness an unfolding of magic.
A truth, a reflection, a beauty, a calling to ourselves.
The dance of being seen.

This is written for the unheard generation.
For the little boys who are lost, misplaced, alone,
cornered by darkness walking into light.
For the men framed inside the child Goliath.

Inspired by my nephew Ricky Jr.
Dedicated to Ricky Jr., Jonier, Omar, Daniel, and Jose Antonio.

O.P.B.

I brought flowers and donuts
to my friends today, for the coffee that
was served in fine China along
with stories you can't find anywhere.

On this street, the rainbow of children ran
through the corridors of the old brick building.

My neck bending time and time again to
reach their extended arms.

Laughter seeps from within the walls where we gather.
Today, my friends sat in a circle on worn-out chairs.
We listened to music while drinking wine and beer.

My eyes study the strength of these hardworking women
realizing that at times the solidarity and
shared secrets are thicker than blood.

Escaping to join this tribe of humbled energy
filled with humility and common ground.

Those days when I exit towards their homes,
I lived treasured moments for which my friends I owe.

*Dedicated to the gatherings in the parking lot
on Oakland Park Blvd. with Magda, Vanessa, and Ana Liz.*

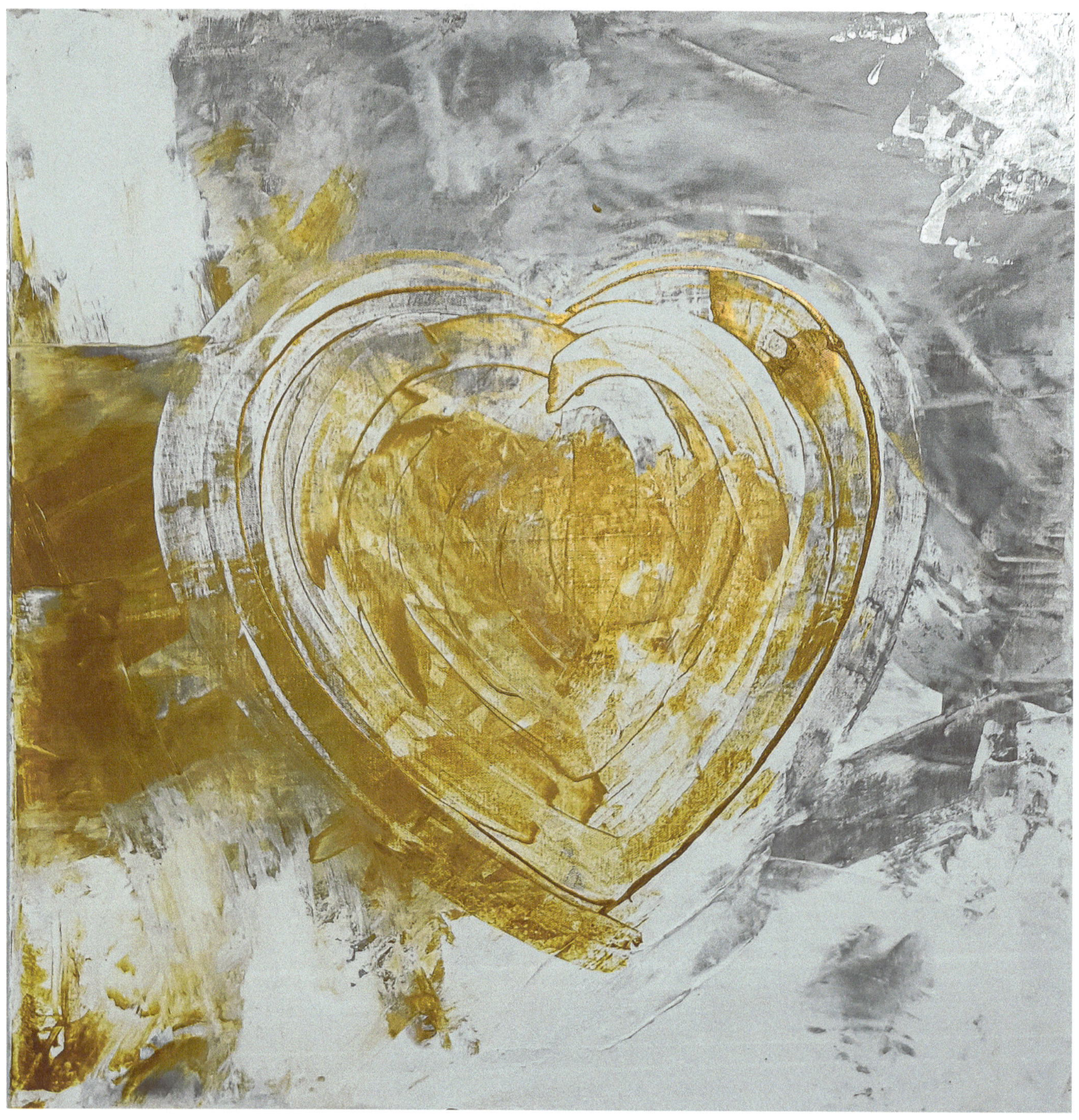

BEAUTIFUL GRACES

I came from a sight of soaring dreams
blazing trails of triumphs.

I saw the power of desire go calculated
with precision to win.

The pride of little women with a song of victory
in their hearts and hope beaming on their faces.

I saw her extend her wings, rising to
unbeatable heights, balancing the winds of adversity
while defining the essence of strength
she doesn't even know she has.

I saw graces come from different horizons
no goal is too big or too far for these
girls with the gold mine of youth and resilience.

I saw such bold and beautiful souls of a
tomorrow so promising.
I saw such wonderful things.

*Inspired by my niece, Jennifer, and her friends at
a gymnastics competition, ages 12-15.
Dedicated to all young girls aspiring to become.*

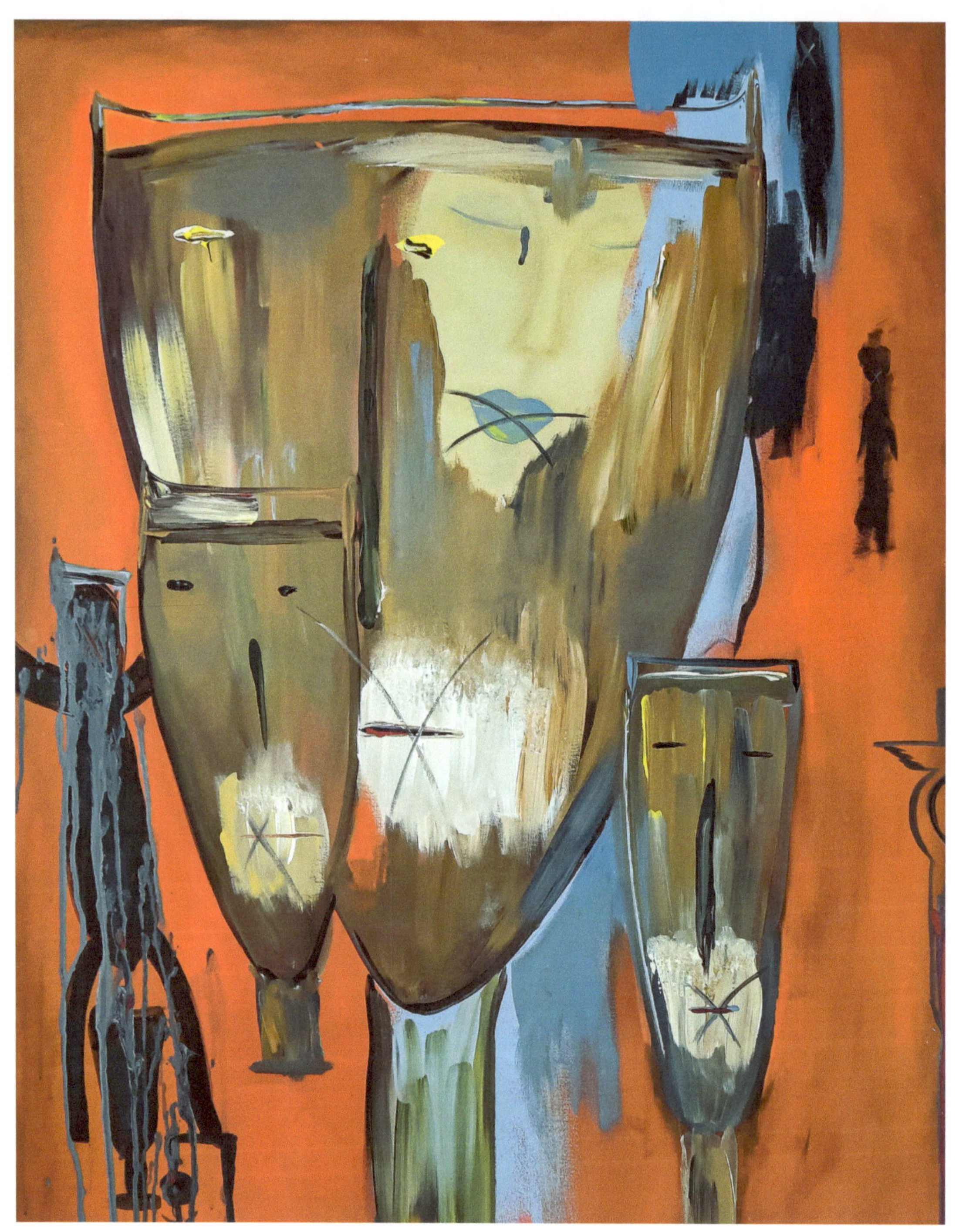

COLD FEET

Cringed brows push thoughts to the edge
like a spilling volcano.
Streams of blood, love, and life
poured out from within that girl,
afraid of the mind that has restricted the waves of
Womanhood, Motherhood, Christhood.

As the veins empty, her insides wrestle to nestle
themselves with a foreign exchange of promise.

Cradled in despair a moment of release,
for every pain of rebirth, the story repeats,
for every memory, a minute of silence to grieve,
for every drop an answer of hope to alleviate the cries.

The dreadful encounter with that lifeless anatomy,
violated by instruments warmed with irony
buried with no say, fear was left to control.

There swelled anger withholding, mending a punctured
wound placed in the sacred place of miracles
and journeys robbed from their homes and functions.

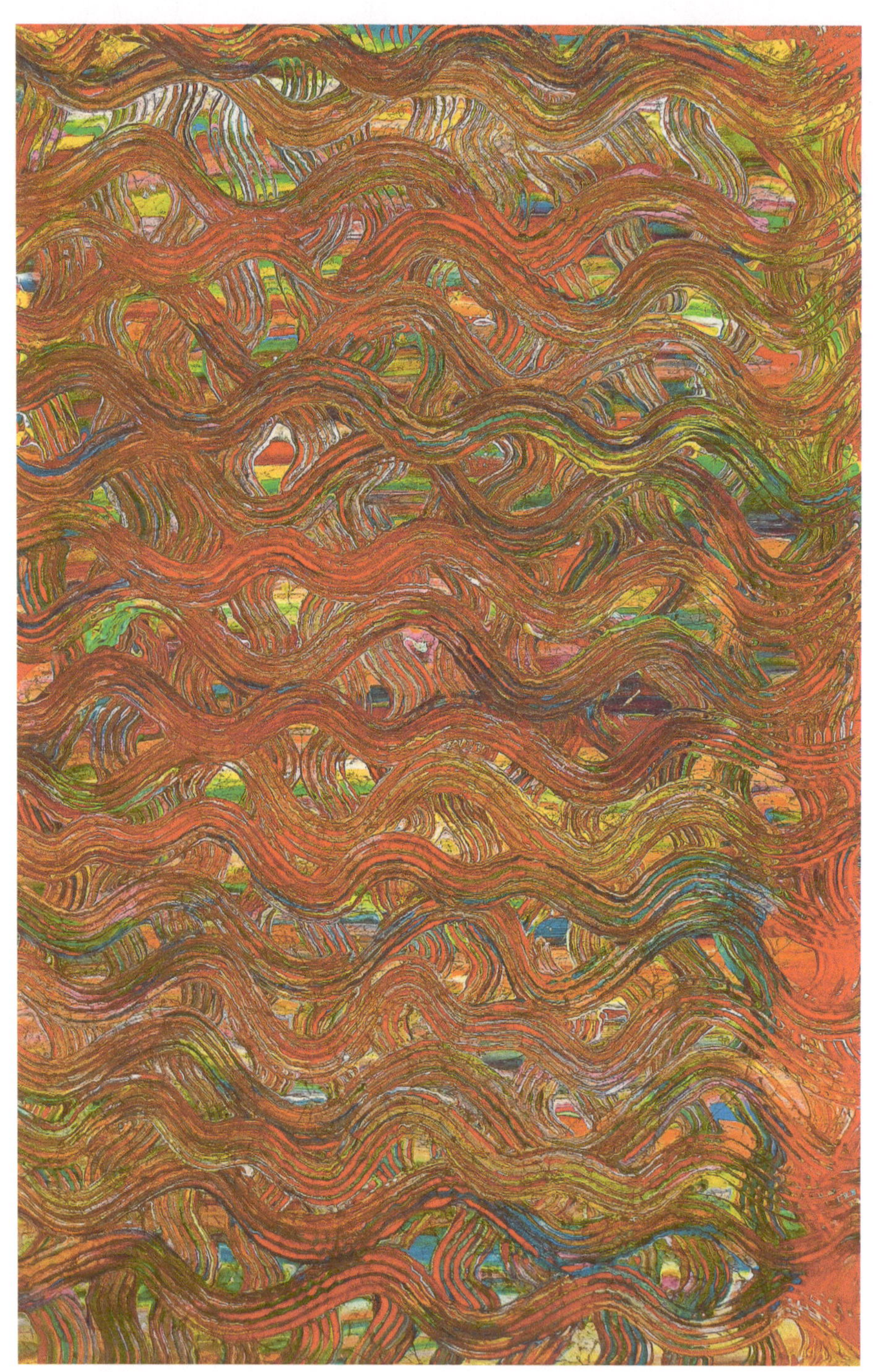

CIRCLES IN THE SAND

My lover called me under a Crescent moon,
the burning sage lighting up the circles
drawn in the sand.

Engraving words to manifest,
I sit at the center facing east.
The shaving of drenched bark mixed
in bowls that carry moon water,
blessed for rituals performed by prophets
eating bread loaded with seeds hidden for
the harvest of September.

The initiatives that call the masses into academic attics
where I once stood naked before an easel
scribed with words like tolerance and safe.

The desk covered with ashes of Nag Champa
revealed the ceremonies of community healing.
Painting a canvas of meadows, emeralds, turquoise,
and pale shades of chalked blue that drip
a sublime kaleidoscope onto a grave.

*Inspired by a professor's academic studies
on diverse initiatives and his love for the moon manifestation.*

I AM GONE

The quilted mantle spreads across the floor waiting
to cape my bare back,
a sweet scent of amber and
ocean spray seeped into its fabric.

My spirit melted into its trance.
I became one with the patterned peacocks.
Dancing around the tree, I am the tree
that oozes the ache a medicinal healing can bring,
only by the index of the one who anoints my staff.

The smells enchant me and the sounds of drumming
pounding in my heart, racing to escape the walls
I built around sanctioned memories.
I am robed with colors of prayers as I chant…
I am gone.
I am Shiva Ham.

Walking on glistening sand spotlighted by the moon
on my way to marinate in waters
filled with schools of wisdom you can only get here.

Inspired by full moon walks on the South Carolina coast.

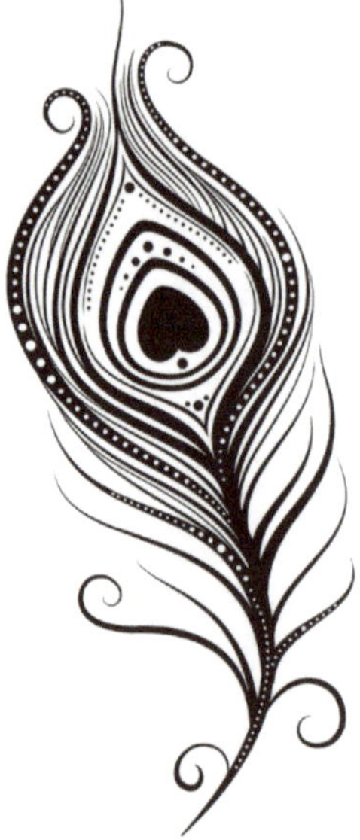

INDIFFERENCE

My heart beats at a pace where I can feel
the pause in between the counts.
Relieved because I finally understood
what it was saying.

I can feel my lips smiling to itself, hearing
the echoing of written prophecies.

The sun resting on my cheeks celebrated
my mind pausing, and there I heard the children laugh.
My feet felt the grass and welcomed fallen leaves,
everything was knitted so perfectly.

Gratitude fills my lungs; my hands hold each other.

Feeling the warranty of life as I nestled my face,
that only feels the tender nurturing.

Being.

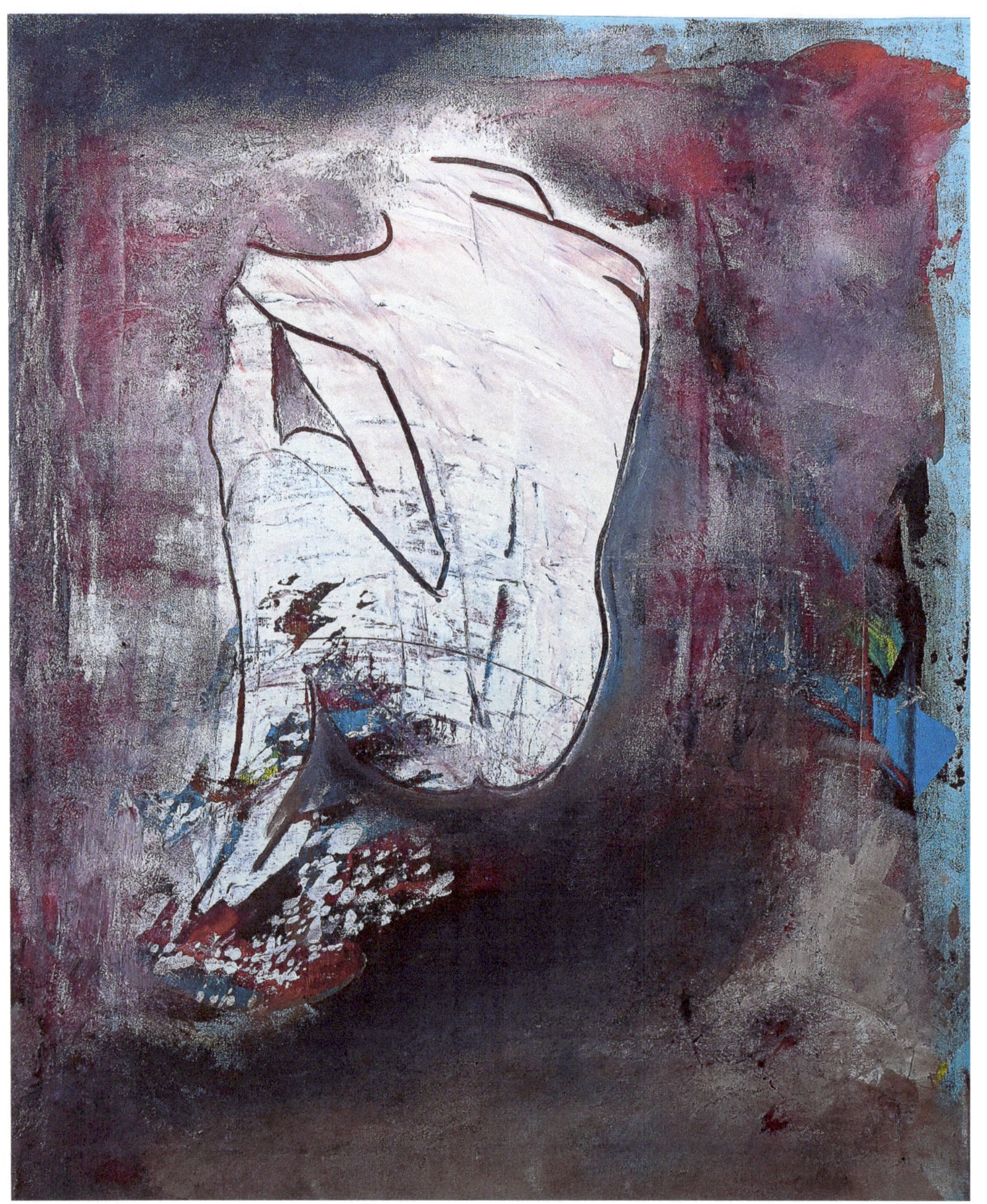

TEMPLES HOME

What precious temple raveled by the pains
filmed on x-ray sheets.

Lift me into the warm song of solace caressing the tilted height,
shifting currents of waves signaling for help.

I have not forgotten the pain felt by the struggles carried out
on stormy days, nor the burns marking my feet
from the deadweight dragged around.

Let the power of healing rush to soothe you.
A perfection of truth that never changes
but is forgotten and misused.

You are whole, made from the breath of all good.
You have carried me, my faithful obedient servant.
The unconscious elements sailing
will no longer wither this perfect form.

We will be the flight of the horizon, a brilliant star,
the screams of joy, a respite voice to call home.

We will be our testimony.

Ode to my body and the journey of a boat accident
fracturing my back and the struggle to regain strength.

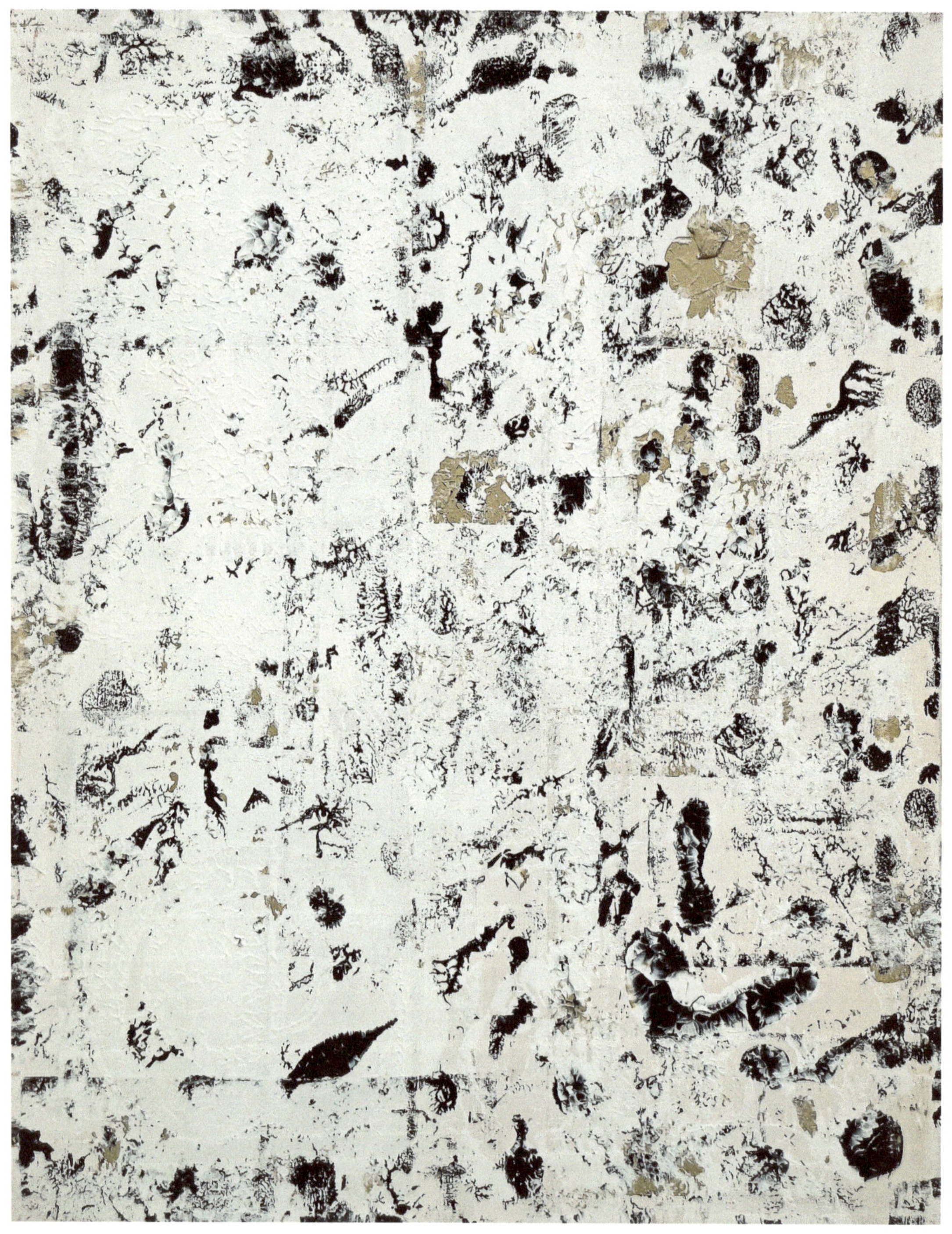

HOLDING

The house is empty but for the ghost of judgments,
phasing out positioned listening,
she screams to let go of prized comforts,
and hidden agendas that generate dormant feuds.

Not realizing that a deaf ear stand
before its short circuits.
The bleeding from thorns pulled out of our eyes and, frozen fingers
from pointing have numbed us.

Why have we harbored thoughts residing
in aging wounds of survival?
Why the reckless proclaims of insistent assumptions
cited by thoughts that mortgage our future?
Why doesn't the music man sing
precious and fragile things?

The silence reflects the resistance with futile depths of right and wrong.
Unwilling to serve each other allowances for uncommon grounds,
all the while tangled in our manacles afraid, and
refusing to knock on heaven's door.

We are of no correction. There is no place for knowing.
Clarity is chilled in swirls of tasty colors
savored in moments when sharing and holding
become our safety.

Look at us, paralyzed in our perception of one another.
A painting filled with fury and ghosts floating on red seas.
What if we knew nothing and loved simply?

Dedicated to the music man.

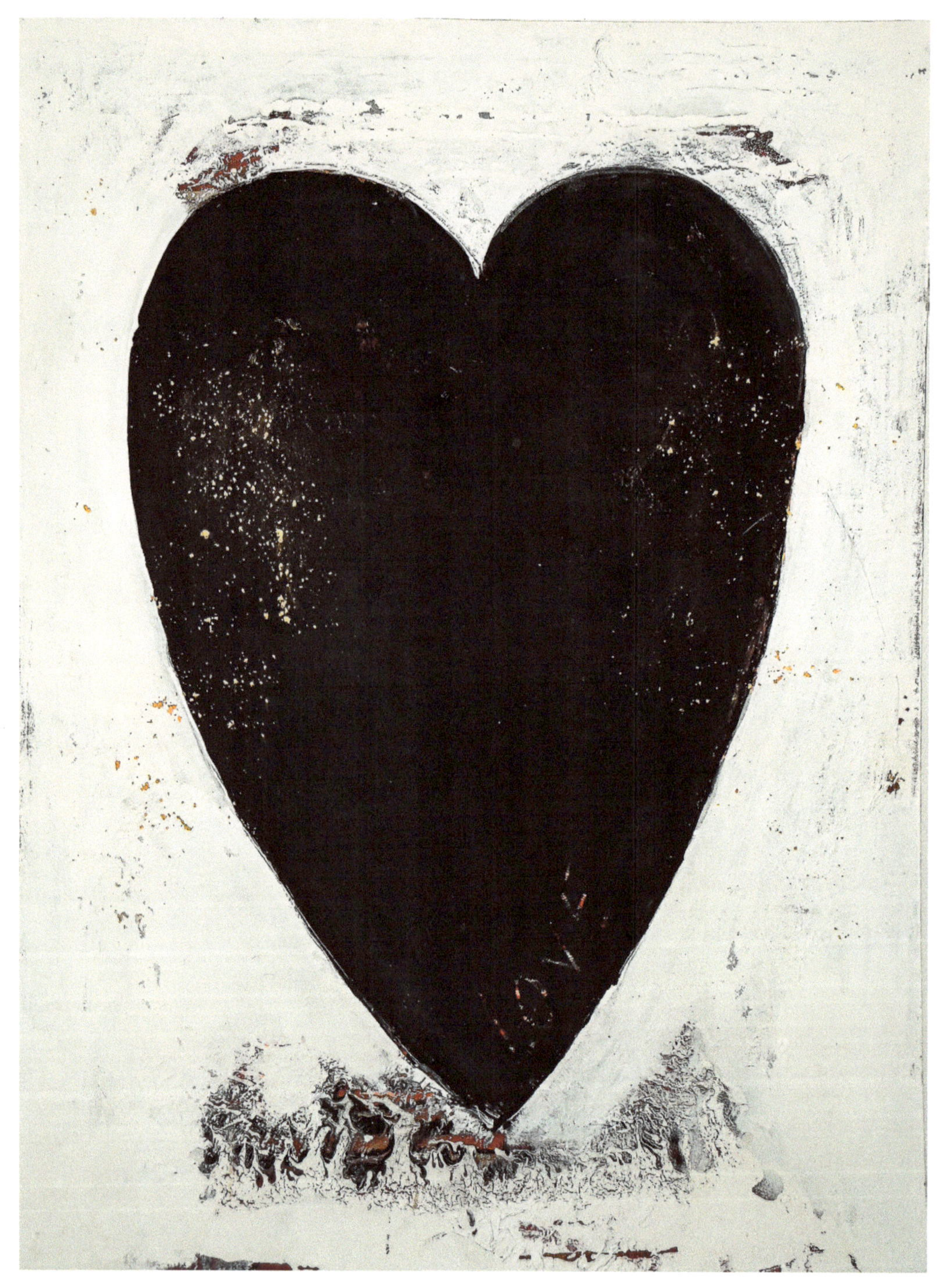

AUGUST

Crystal lights are glittering the sky
Seagulls dance across the bridge from city to city.
Polluted air sends a tasteless breeze
while the deep waters rock me.

I am filled with sorrow, dried out
like the soil beneath my little trees back home.
Summer has not seen me and trails of these dragging feet
illuminate the cold halls of this deserted ward.

The unforeseen avalanche swept us all,
entering a madness of colliding uncertainties.
Her face was struck by explosive pressure
built from past consciousness that caught up to us all.

And all I knew was that she would bear witness to these times.

The nights are still, my heart dangling
from my mother's aching body as I bathe her frail skin.
I think of these rewarding photographed moments
that have been recorded in me.

I weep in silence as the night falls,
and in that August, we aged together.

*Written in the halls of a Maryland Hospital where my mother
recovered from a near-fatal car accident.*

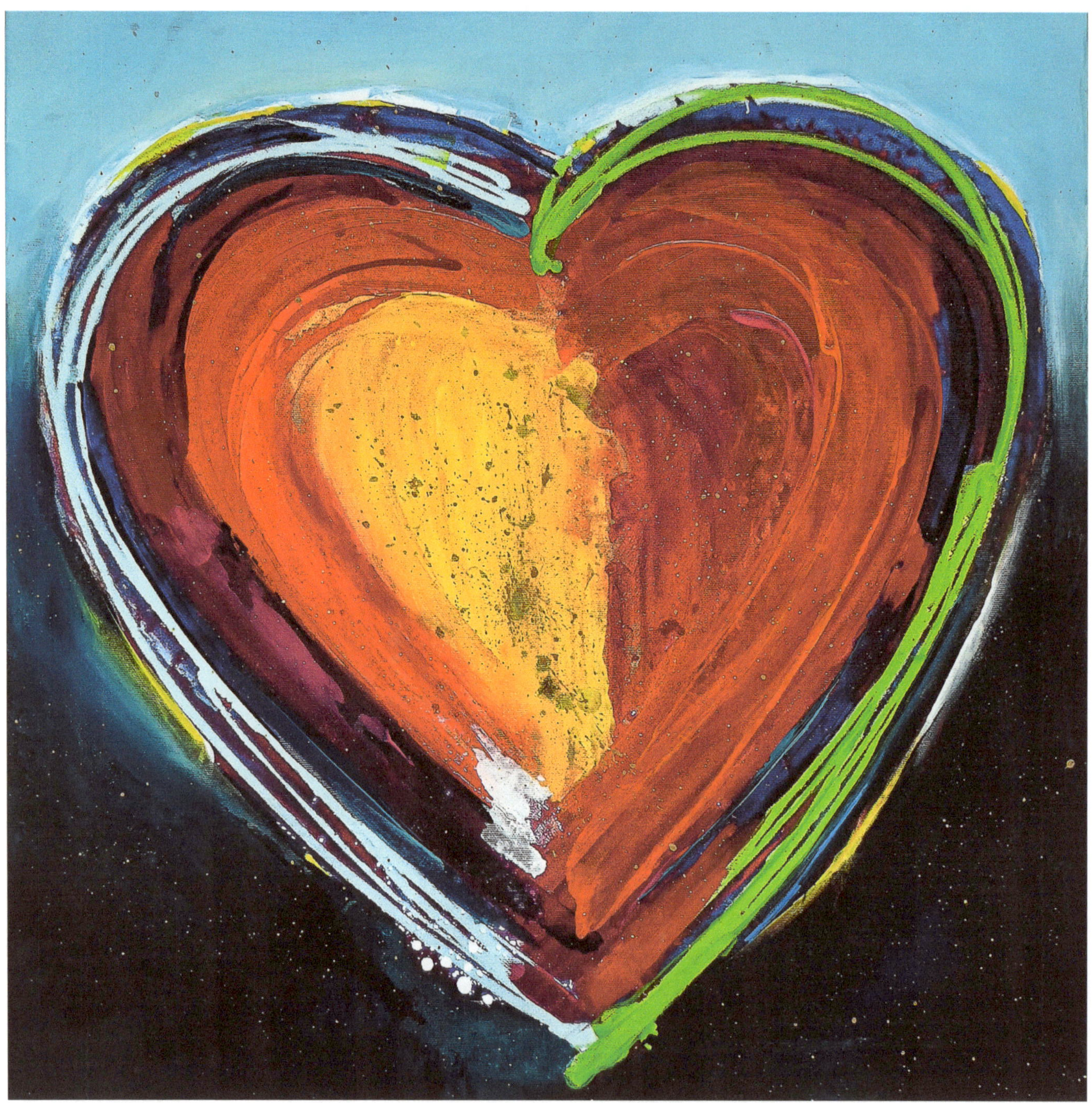

ALWAYS

Blowing breeze I tremble under siege.
The mind's discordance goes deep,
waiting for my soft surrender.

Pulled by startled wind, I weep, lost in your heavens.
Drenched in oceans altered by foreign activities
contrast to the awakening.
I linger on this resisted heart.

Cloaked by dangerous shadows.
Led by the rebel within.

I stand by you, my God,

My every mention of sound.
My clear sight.
My warranty of joy.

My peace, you are always.

My Prayer

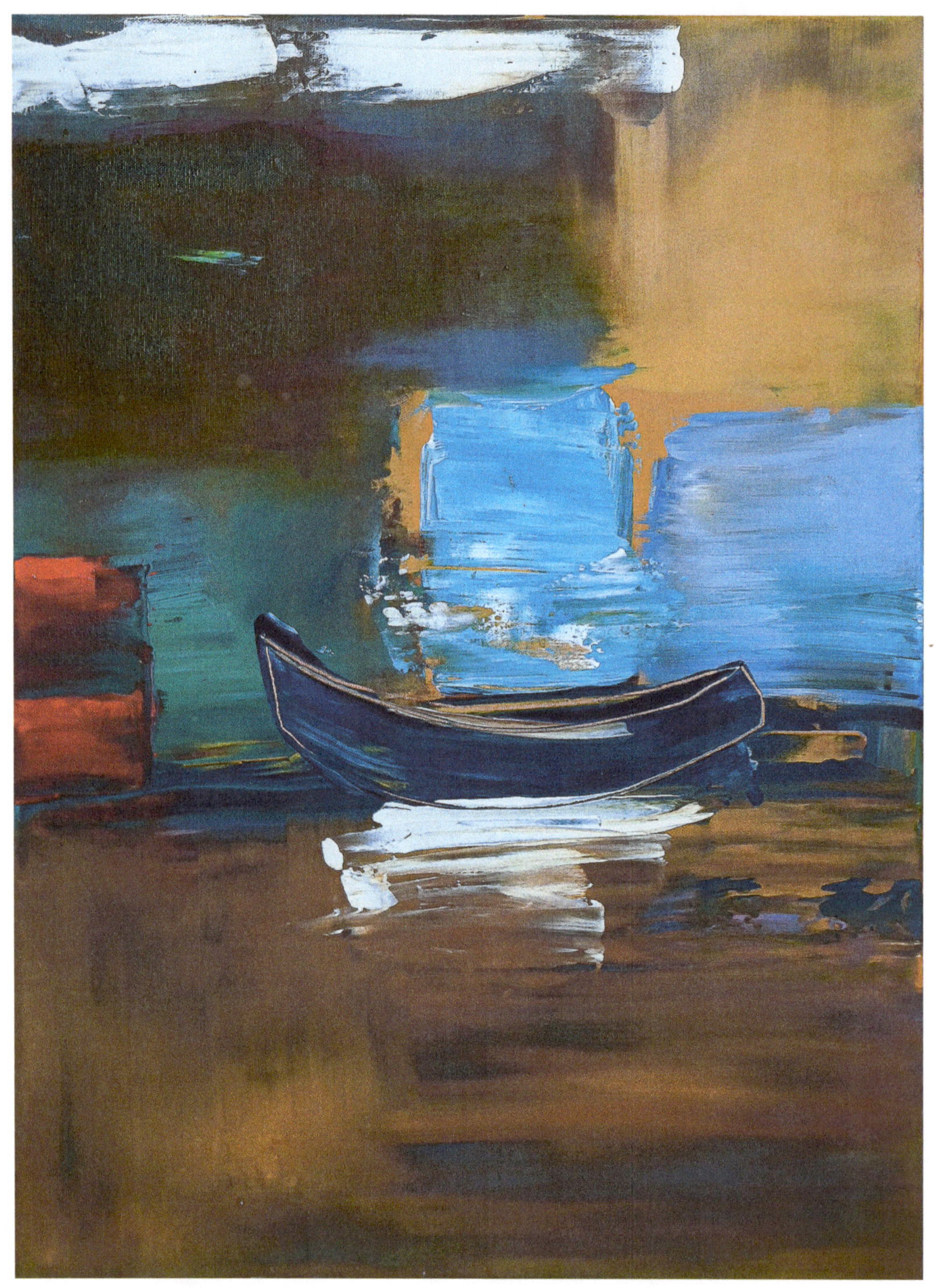

LIFEBOAT

You are not here.
No one is speaking to me.
The hurt I hear echoes from the depth of past lives haunting me.
My mind trying to sweep up the specks of dust,
busies itself with mundane tasks to avoid being.

Scared to stand in truth that I throw away my vote for living,
believing awards are given to those with martyred anthems.

I yearn to sit in the dirt long enough to feel the earth calling.
I crave freedom from my discomforts,

I pull out the sweet thorn in the side of my dead weight,
waiting to rise from abandoned life stories.

I stand to envision the waters mending the world's hurts.
I pledge to save the drowning from giving up on themselves,
the distracted from getting lost.

You are not here. You speak to no one but yourself.
The hurt you feel comes from past lives waiting to be let go.
If we don't stand in the truth of who we are and vote to live,
we gain nothing and lose it all.

Inspired by one of the most transformational exercises
I experienced during my Summit Education training.

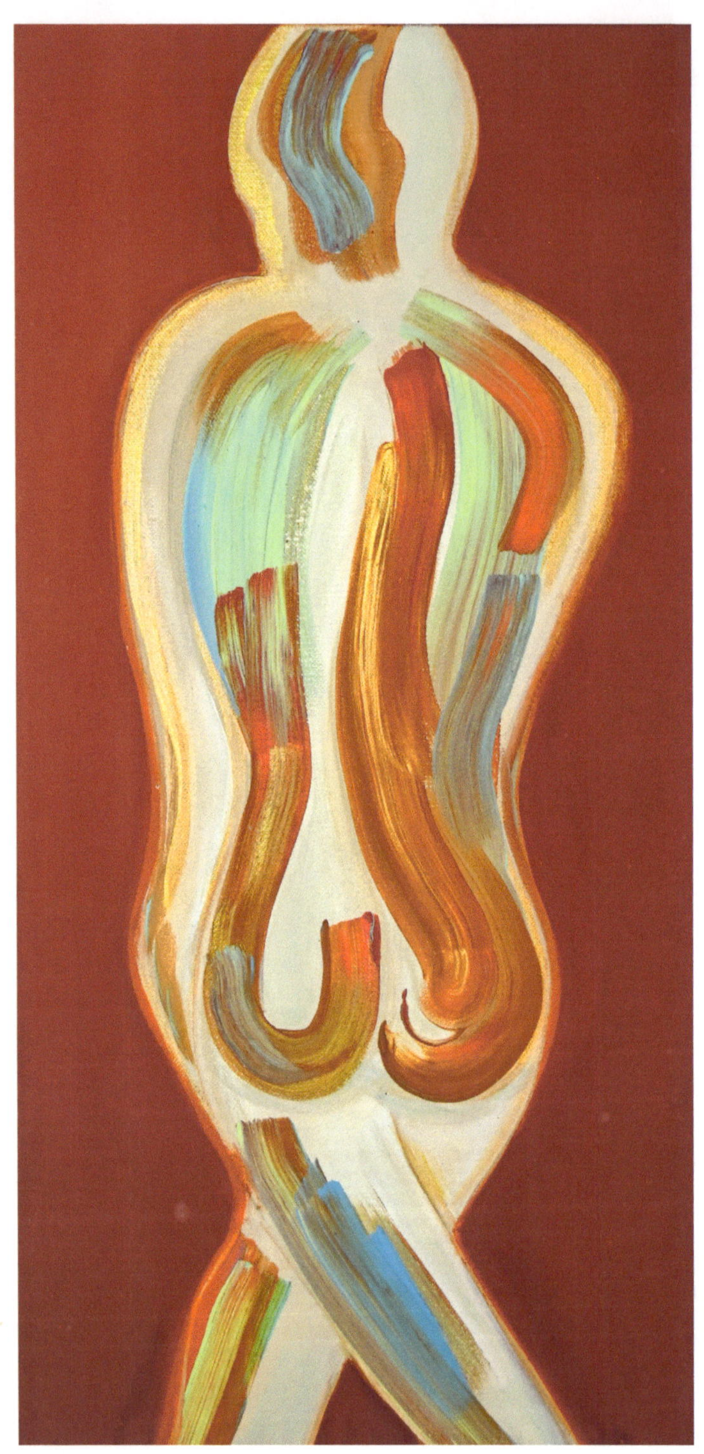

*I never saw a wild thing sorry for itself. A
small bird will drop frozen dead from a
bough without ever having felt sorry for itself.*

—D. H. Lawrence

RUNNING

The wind makes me lucid as I fly through
sharp edges targeting me.

I steady my pace vanishing
to a weathered shelter where I can
mend from the brush fires.

Awake and scared, no rest for this
gazelle's heart beating fast, living
caved yet safe.

Waiting for the morning sun to
touch me so I can run again, fly again.
Be free again.

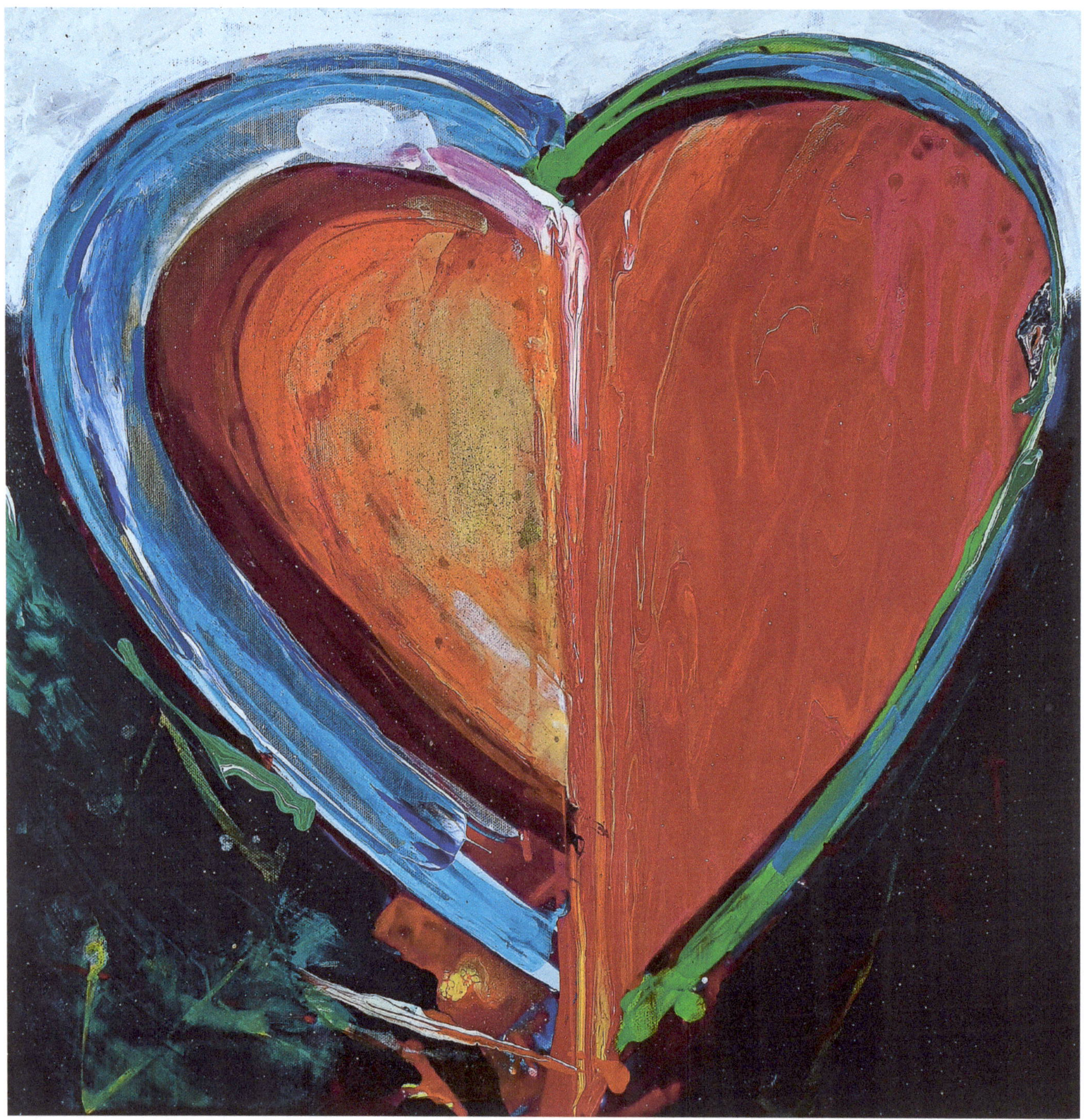

HURTING

Oh, my tormented soul imprisoned by angst,
slaved by critics and enthusiasts.

Stewing with burden, all while searching
for a connection tethered to Source.

A dread for the world's condition that keeps me up,
offering help while avoiding what I dare not fathom.

I am still keeping steady for this heart that I
find fragile and frightful.

Believing that my part is enough and
sleep can become my friend again.

This deep earth echoing to be rescued,
these children's cries and trembles recorded in my head.

These defenseless creatures in hiding
are a weight so grim to bear.

For the defenseless animals and children of the world.

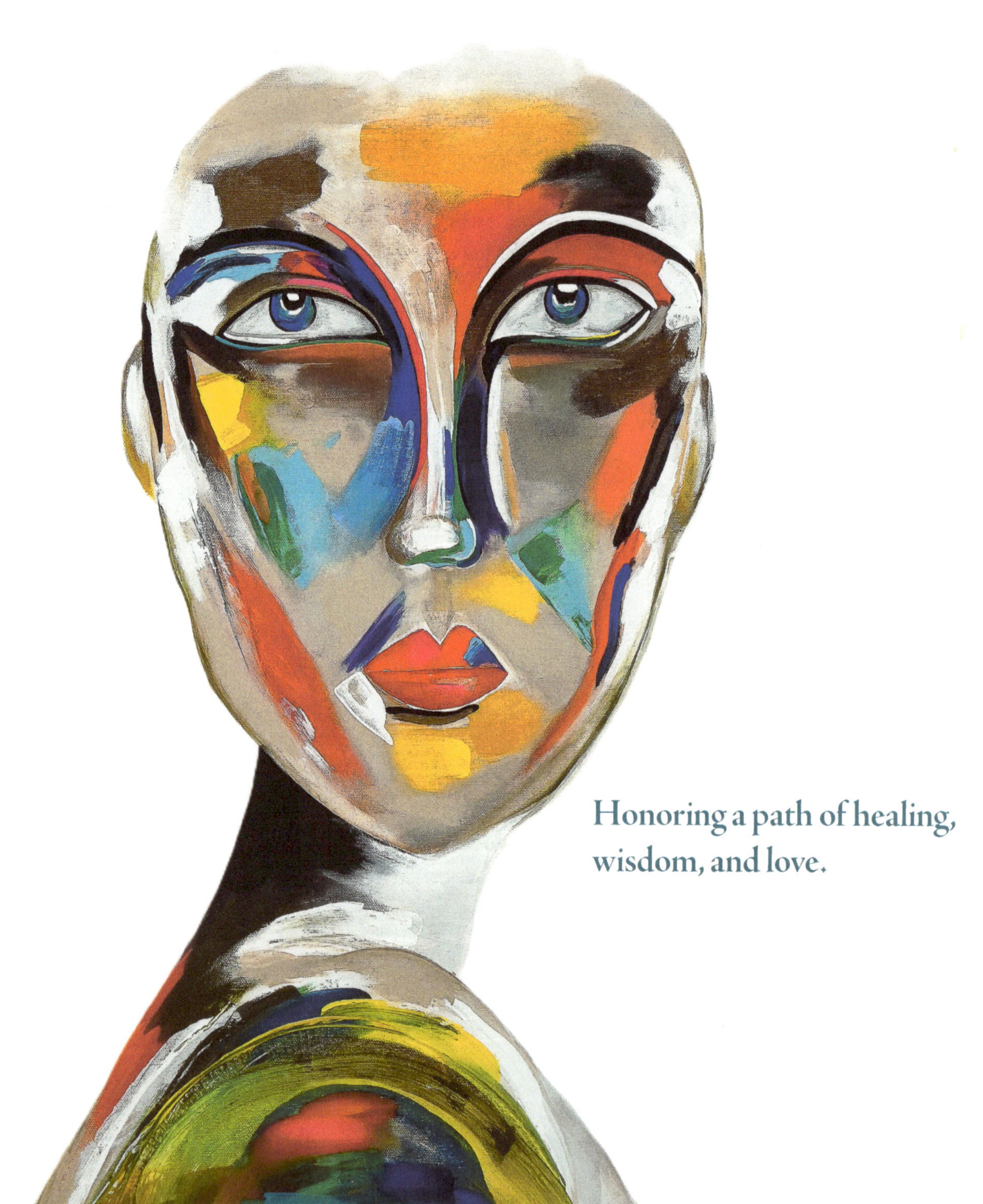

Honoring a path of healing,
wisdom, and love.

STABLE

A call for peace within, seeking truth as bitterness dissolves.
I am jumping through hoops just to find my anchor.

Waiting to reap without growing weary,
I stretch my old self thin
anticipating the breakthrough that will redefine me.

It's an old song of yesterday's limitations, a dance around
the same graves, a whistle to the sound of atonement,
and a stance to intersect it all.

I'm divorcing this old, recycled consciousness.
I am exposing the unhealed flesh to be made whole with higher vibrations.

Climbing the mountain in retreat from crossed boundaries,
to enter a silence that is resounding, to walk the
labyrinth of contemplation to an insight unknown.

Life is so fickle, and it moves with no regard, trying to
keep up with tomorrow's learning when I haven't
even got the lesson of the day. Who can master the
ever changing condition of spoiled thoughts?
Trying to make the right choice.

God keep me stable in your word and hardcore
in self-awareness. Build me back to that place of innocence
where a little girl once roamed.

Written for my warrior's heart's love for herself.

ACKNOWLEDGMENTS

I am blessed to have connections with amazing people who have empowered and inspired me
throughout my life.

To my 3 a.m. lifetime friendships

Diane, mi amiga del alma, I don't know of anyone with a more giving heart than yours. Thank you for always being so present
in my life and for the amazing adventures we had flying the friendly skies. Thank you for believing in every one of my dreams,
and crazy ideas. Gracias por tu Amistad.

Orlando, my coffee poetry partner our special bond as artists and friends has made my life much richer. 3 West Production
was there when it all started. Thank you for holding me in your heart, and for our wonderful friendship that has kept us going
through life's ups and downs.

Kevin, my Imu, thank you for your unconditional support and Love. For believing in the artist in me before I believed in
myself. For lighting the way to Spiritual awakenings and introducing me to the world of transformation. I am honored to have
been part of some of your historical life moments and grateful that you are part of mine.

Teri-Lynn, I remember my forever coaching buddy and best friend, who never let me run it for more than 5 minutes and held
my hand while I got off whatever troubled me. You are in my heart every day.

Monikah, Breakthrough could not look more beautiful than our friendship. For all the brainstorming all-nighters creating
something out of nothing. For always asking the hard questions and holding a space where we get to be girls and Queens at
the same time while adjusting each other's crowns. Doctora, thank you for your steady voice on nights when mine trembled
and for bringing me back to center with your calm.

Derek, for being a constant stand in my life, and for teaching me to see beyond people's choices and value who they are. How
fortunate am I to have the brilliance of your coaching and the care and genuine love of a gentle giant who took me under his
wing to share his love for photography. May we always remind each other to #loveemanyway, thank you for the music.

Gali, my Goddess sister, for your love and friendship and the reminder that self-care is vital and the journey to the moon is
smoother when we are open to illumination and release.

Greg, for showing me the joy and love of bathing in the light of the moon. You will always be the medicine man to me. Thank you for teaching me to create circles in the sand stepping into my heart's calling. For keeping our connection as sacred as the fashionable cool hat-wearing cat that you are, Aho Mitakuye Oyasin.

Brigitte, what a blessing to call you my sister friend. You have defined that laughter is truly the best medicine. Your heart of gold shines everywhere you go, and I am grateful to know you have my back no matter what. Love you, girl! #shovelpartners

Jeff, my Pot of Gold thank you for being the safe shoulder to cry on while our laughter dried those same tears, and being the hand that held mine tightly while life took a sharp turn. #Jonathanlivingstonseagulls

Maxine Groves, a life coach with a heart of gold Thank you for your insightful wisdom and for all the times you said yes to meeting up with me to guide, listen, and call me out to recognize my greatness I admire and love you 444

Dr. Elizabeth King, you are the epitome of strength and determination. Thank you for sharing your journey and allowing me to capture the historical moments that the SSL Foundation creates. Your community outreach is a constant inspiration. Thank you for modeling for me what being fearless and unstoppable looks like.

Abuela, gracias por ser el ejemplo de Fortaleza y servicio. Por siempre ayudar a tus vecinos y a los enfermos y ensenarme que compartir un plato de comida es una bendicion y honor. Te amo y te extraño.
Mi Familia y Amigos de Puerto Rico, la riqueza, bendicion y amor que siento por ustedes es inmenso, los quiero infinitamente.

My UTC Family, the teachings, lessons, opportunities, and friendships I have made are priceless. Reverend Charles Taylor, for teaching truth principles in a way everyone gets. Reverend Anna Price for the wisdom you bring to every class and sermon. Reverend Lottie Clodfelter for encouraging me to write. Nerissa Street for creating the Inspirational Poetry Café, and Reverend Jackelyn Hazel for teaching me the power of forgiveness.

Titi Ita, thank you for all the love and care you have always shown us, and for being there for me when I needed a cup of coffee and an understanding heart. You are very special to me.

My American Airlines friends, my time with you in the friendly skies has been some of my most amazing experiences and memorable moments. I thank each one of you who sat alongside me during take-off and each safe landing, I miss you all. Some of my poetry was written right there on that jump seat alongside you.

ACKNOWLEDGMENTS *(cont'd)*

The Summit Education Community, Ken, and Kathy my life will forever be positively transformed because of your stand for the city. Thank you for opening a space for Discovery, Breakthrough, and Mastery but most of all for the awareness that standing for myself, and others is the ultimate path to an extraordinary world of possibilities.

To the incredible **transformational teachers** I called into my experience, some who kicked my ass straight into my power. John Hanley Jr., Kathy Benson, Ray Blanchard, Chris Lee, Betty Spruill, and Michael Strasner, I thank you all for your stand. Thank you, Jo Englesson, for building a community where Luis got to fly.

My IDA Family, home away from home, thank you for embracing me with such love and kindness. Coming to work for an organization that values family, education and the art of Dance has been a true blessing.

Luis, you will forever be my greatest mirror. Thank you for reminding me that "I must be the change I wish to see." For the amazing ride and adventures taken with your Passionate, Courageous, and Trusting Spirit that has made an everlasting impact on my heart. For sharing a beautiful home and space where I got to dream and fly. I love you dearly. #peasinapod

To some of the **great poets** of our time who transported me with spoken word and inspired me to write. Julia De Burgos, Khalil Gibran, EE Cummings, Emily Dickinson, Edgar Alan Poe, Maya Angelou, W.B. Yeats, Pablo Neruda, Rudyard Kipling, Walt Whitman, and D.H. Lawrence, to name a few.

To my brilliant friends: Monikah Ogando, Kevin K. Ross, Orlando Rodriguez, and Uncle Japhet Zayas, who happen to be amazing writers and accomplished published authors and poets, for their unwavering support throughout this project. Thank you.

ABOUT THE AUTHOR

Rhonda Gutierrez is a professional artist, originally from the Bronx, New York, currently residing in Miramar, Florida. Rhonda's approach to art is ambitious: she seeks to transcend the aesthetic elements of art by employing a holistic technique that creates an atmosphere conducive to our connectedness and capacity to heal.

Whether poetry, photography, or painting, a common unifying thread runs through Rhonda's creations: our interrelatedness. This human factor drives her global approach to art: art for art's sake; art for man's sake; art for the world's sake.

Her ever-expanding search for new artistic vistas is evident in her eclectic entries in local exhibits and competitions. Rhonda's primary means of artistic expression--portrait photography--showcases her ability to create a trusted space where family, friends, and clients surrender themselves to discover their voices through her lens.

Rhonda does not limit herself to captured images. The influence of Picasso, de Kooning, Pollack, and Klee graces her canvases. Her use of line, texture, shape, and color further explores their interpretations of reality to come together in her unique style. Rhonda's original paintings, photographs, and Giclee prints are available through her Miramar, Florida studio. Her photographs have appeared on book covers and published content.

A PERSONAL NOTE

I write and paint because it is my sincerest way of self-expression and how I interpret my experiences.

It took me a while to share my talents and gifts with others as I lacked confidence in my work. With the love and encouragement of many, I found my voice and added color to it. The greatest lesson learned through this discovery has been the opportunity to explore new connections that have been invaluable in my life.

Writing and reading poetry for me is entering a world with no limits, no judgments, just the simple enjoyment of words coming together.

Sharing my poetry with you has been a vulnerable and cherished journey to which I am grateful. Hoping you find the freedom of expression in your own life and strive to hold on to its ultimate fulfillment.

The biggest gift to myself has been leaning into the pain of discomfort for the sake of personal growth and self-love, which has been the theme of this book. Trusting God and exercising my spiritual muscles have kept me moving steadily and faithfully even when I am being still.

Namaste,

—Rhonda

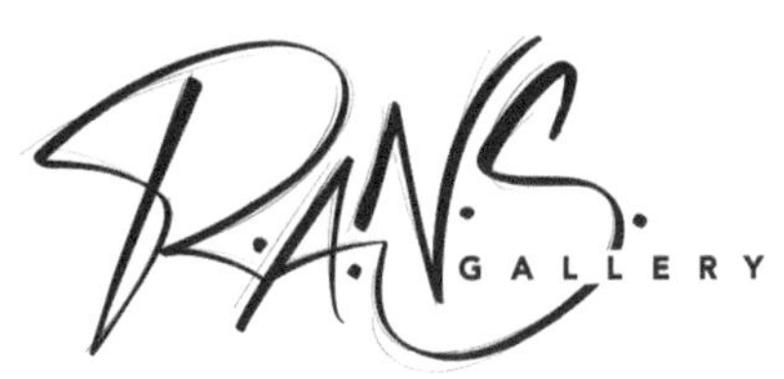

www.ingramcontent.com/pod-product-compliance
Lightning Source LLC
LaVergne TN
LVHW061116240125
801961LV00003B/7